STOP SELLING!
SERVE
AND GET PAID WHAT YOU'RE WORTH

BERNARD QUISUMBING

Cover Design and Layout
Susi Clark of 2 Peak Publishing & Creative Blueprint Design

Contributor
Tammie Chrin of 2 Peak Publishing | www.instagram.com/2PeakPublishing.com

CONTENTS

FOREWORD

Life can be a joyful, fun and an adventurous experience, when everything is going your way. Then out of nowhere, disaster strikes! It could be a small event, or a sea change, and you go from "King of the Hill" to the bottom of the barrel. Maybe even sinking into a deep rut that's difficult to get out of. From a positive and fun experience of life to a negative and painful one. Has this happened to you yet? Have you experienced the ups and downs in your life, the minor setbacks to a big crash?

When life does not seem to be going your way, we often become angry, hurt, sad, disappointed, and even discouraged or depressed. How have you reacted to unforeseen calamity like this the past? Some people resort to drinking, drug abuse, addiction and isolation from others to cope with such negative and painful feelings. The pain is real, and it can be debilitating!

In his book, "STOP SELLING! Serve, and Get Paid What You're Worth," Bernard shares his life's journey openly, with vulnerability and lays it all on the line for the reader. As you'll read, Bernard's life was a mess…a big mess!

Sometimes in life, there are outside forces that cause bad things to happen to us. In Bernard's case, his initial reactions to these negative forces added to the pain and the misery. Bernard was going downhill fast.

I know what you're thinking at this point. What does this have to do with selling, about serving, or even making lots of money? Well, Bernard's misfortune and destructive choices have very little to do with the specific steps involved in selling properly; like choosing the right word track when describing a product's features and benefits.

However, the way Bernard came to learn his approach to such challenges in life has everything to do with being successful and prosperous in the profession of selling. In many ways, the Inner Game of selling is the process of learning to successfully approach challenges.

These grand themes of service and approaching challenges in life and selling, are illuminated and made real here. Bernard's journey delves deep into his own personal bleak and desperate challenges in life, and in selling. Through his miraculous discovery of certain core principles, forged in these challenges, a new wisdom and personal power is shared for us all to benefit from.

Like the wonderful teacher Robert Schuller said, "bloom where you're planted." Bernard took action where he landed, when it wasn't easy, and when conditions were certainly not perfect.

Despite our own challenges and imperfect conditions, especially when practicing the art of selling, the use of the timeless principles and steps found in Bernard's story give us all a path forward to getting paid what we're worth. From baby steps to big bold steps; from the uncomfortable to the fun, there is a wealth of personal experience and knowledge here for anyone.

This is one man's path; from a "broken ship" to "cruising in style". Bernard unlocked an inner attitude of service, of being unstoppable, so he could get paid what he was worth in the car business, and find true success in life, with his family, and in his passions. I believe you can too, in whatever endeavor you are faced with, and Bernard's story can help!

As you read this book, I hope you are inspired to adopt and apply the golden nuggets Bernard shares in order to take your step-by-step journey to transform your life, accomplish your goals, and reach heights of success that you may never have thought possible.

Tom Pearce
Sales Coaching Group

INTRODUCTION

If you're looking for a technically-skilled training manual on how to manipulate your customers, use outdated, cheesy closing lines, or high-pressure-squeeze your clients into buying your products, this book is NOT for you. However, if you're looking for some amazing tips on how to raise your game, serve your customers to the very best of your ability, get paid handsomely, and live a very successful, content, and grateful life in sales, then I promise you that you will find gems in the upcoming chapters.

With 13 years in the car business, I've experienced all of the ups and downs of the salesman's life. From working 60–70 hour weeks, taking calls at all hours of the night, missing birthday parties, weddings, and other family events that fell on a Saturday, to crushing sales goals, winning awards, and taking home huge paychecks and bonuses, I was a student of the game. I studied and researched my products like a madman. I also did a lot of research on the competitive brands to see what my cars were up against. I've spent thousands of hours reading or listening to sales books upon sales books... improving my closing techniques from aligning myself with authors like Zig Ziglar, Grant Cardone, J. Douglas Edwards, Joe Verde, Joe Girard, and so many more... .

I've had good months, and I've had bad ones. I've experienced amazing, record breaking months, and I've felt the pain and stress of the slowest, mind-numbing, dead crawl of a winter one. I've also gone through months of selling in desperation, just praying that I'd make enough to cover my bills, as well as flying through months selling with so much money in my bank account, that it didn't even matter to me if I made any sales at all. For the majority of my early years as a salesman, life was a constant roller coaster. However, God had a different plan for me. I've made millions of mistakes and was given even more second chances. I've gone through trials and tests, passes and failures, and have learned countless lessons. Through them all, I now live an amazing, fruitful life of abundance... living a very low-stress, super enjoyable life being a husband and a father, and taking care of thousands of happy customers. The best part of all of it is this: I've kept track of all of these underlying lessons, digging deeper into them, mapping them, learning and unlearning concepts, mining out the diamonds, and really finding a deeper understanding until I found the profound answers or meanings within them... and that's exactly what I want to share with you in this book!

CHAPTER 1
BORN SALESMAN

Now if you're thinking you have to be born a salesman, with the killer instincts or personality to be super successful at sales, let me just destroy that myth right now! I was definitely not born a salesman! Actually, when I first got hired, I was utterly horrible! I struggled with all of the insecurities that most inexperienced people face jumping into a commission-only-sales-job. I was scared of the customers, and I was scared of some of the managers that I worked for. I didn't want to be too pushy with the clients, and I was always afraid of what the managers would do or say if I messed up a possible deal. Come to think of it, I didn't even plan to be a car salesman.

Let me give you a little backstory. Prior to starting my career in the automotive business, I was a 14-year drug addict, heavily dependent on cocaine and crystal meth. I had moved to Colorado from New Jersey to get away from all of it. At the time, I was 28 years old, unemployed, drug crazed, and up to that point, living in my parent's house as a lazy, overweight freeloader. Yes, I was a meth addict AND overweight. That's how lazy I was. Actually, my mama just loved me a whole lot and fed me about as much as she loved me…. The thing is, my freedom from addiction was nothing short of a miracle, and neither was my invitation to a new life of selling cars!

Here's how it went down! I knew I needed a new life. One that was free from crystal meth, and for some reason, I believed Colorado was the place to go. Supposedly, this was God's country. More importantly, my favorite cousin Missy and her older brother, Raul, lived here so I'll go move in with them! As a drug addict, I really didn't think through my plans. I just went for it, which is one of the qualities that would actually end up helping me out a lot in the future. I remember calling my dad and telling him I was going to go to Colorado to get clean and sober. Note, my dad had always had my back when it came to some of the crazy ideas I had to get clean, so he called me back about an hour later, telling me that he bought me a one-way ticket to Colorado. NEXT WEEK! Needless to say, I was NOT ready for this. I was all talk. But now I had no choice.

I ended up using a lot of meth that last week. I'm talking A LOT a lot. I wanted to go out with a bang and all of my drug dealer friends wanted to send this freeloader off in style. I remember flying into Denver International Airport on October 5th, 2006, still higher than the sky from the night before, eager to start my new life. I had given my dad my last-ever-used meth pipe, and for some weird reason, I had known deep down that this was going to be it for me. When I landed, I called my cousin Missy over and over and over again but she wasn't picking up. I was also barging in on her life as a full blown, over the top meth addict, with tons of baggage, and less than a week's worth of notice. Plus, her older brother Raul told her not to pick up. He was one of those very controlling types that wanted me to end up calling him, so he could direct my next steps in the best ways he knew how.

Now what does any of this have to do with sales? Nothing. It just emphasizes how far I was from being a born salesman when I started, and how possible it is for anyone to become a thriving sales professional, regardless your background... so bear with me just a bit, this gets really good.

Now after 18 hours of me sleeping on one of those god-awful, uncomfortable, hard plastic chairs at the terminal, and over 100 attempts to call Missy, I finally called Raul. He instructed me to take a taxi to a hotel right next to Grace Community Church, the church he and his family went to, and told me to attend the night service designated for young, single members of the congregation. Talk about a first impression. I was closing in on 24 hours since my last hit, and I was crashing hard. Just my luck! And talk about the best way to impress all the single ladies... I ended up falling asleep on the couch, right outside the auditorium, and waking up to all of them exiting after their service ended. Utterly embarrassing!

Steven Duncan, one of the singles at the service, was the super lucky guy that I guess Raul had talked into taking me in for the next few days. Raul had five kids, and didn't really want me in his home with them. I can't really blame him. In the state I was in, I wouldn't want me there neither. So Steve, being a single guy with an apartment and an extra room, agreed to take me in.

He didn't really have anything to worry about though. I spent the next six days in a full crash, sleeping about 22–23 hours per day, only getting up to eat some McDonalds from down the street and use the bathroom to release the waste. During the next few days, Raul and a few friends would come and pray over me. This irritated the crap out of me. I just wanted to sleep and I really wasn't used to people having their hands on my shoulders, praying that Jesus help heal me... but when they left, and it was just me, alone in that room... I prayed. And I said, "Look God, I don't know who or what you are and if you even truly exist, but if You do, You need to take this from me!" I knew at that point that I couldn't do this on my own. Failed rehabs, dozens of quit-to-relapses, and jail time that didn't seem to make a difference, I needed God, the universe, life, SOME THING to take this from me! So I made my first deal! I prayed, "God, if you take this from me, I promise that I will surrender my life to you!"

Six days later, I woke up to the whole room being so bright that I couldn't see anything except faded silhouettes of the bedroom I was in… and I literally felt as though God was pulling the addiction out of me. First, it felt like it was being peeled back from my fingers, up my arms, from my toes, up my legs, and being pulled out from the back of my neck! I knew right then and there that I had finally become free of an addiction that I've been struggling through for over a decade! First thing I did was call my dad to tell him… He cried, I cried… and my life has never been the same.

During this week, Raul was planning on sending me off to another rehab. Not sure anyone was REALLY expecting a miracle like THIS to happen the way it did… but like I said, God had a different plan for me. Soooooo… instead of rehab, I moved into Raul's basement. I became the eldest of his now, six kids. Did I mention he was the controlling type?

I signed a contract filled with rules to live there. Sort of like a lease agreement. But this was all new to me. He also created a spreadsheet with a schedule on how I was to live my life for the next foreseeable future. 5:30 a.m., bible study, 6:30 a.m. get ready for the day, 7 a.m. Breakfast, and out of the house by 7:30 a.m. to go and look for a job, armed with a notebook and a pen. I had to write down all of the places I applied to and jot down the outcomes.

I applied to 43 places in two days… now here's the thing. At that point in my life, the ONLY thing I knew from the Bible was that the truth shall set you free… however, I'd lived the past 10 years of my life being a liar, a manipulator, so I felt as though I had to REALLY STOP LYING if I were to surrender my life to God. Otherwise, this addiction is going to blow right back at me with a force like a hurricane, and that was something I just didn't want to go through any more. I would rather die. Literally.

Sooooo… I filled out my applications. Previous jobs, Drug dealer, drug money collector, and before that, I worked for my parents at Q-Eximtrade doing shipping and receiving. Needless to say, NO ONE HIRED ME! By the third day, I was losing all excitement and motivation. Go figure… That was the same day that Raul decides to tell me, "Today will be the day." What?!?!? How the heck does HE know? As if God told him or something.

Anyway, he was right. Justin Helmick, the new car manager at small, family owned dealership called Denver Isuzu Suzuki on 104th Avenue gave me a shot. The thing is, he pulled me in for an interview BEFORE reading over the application. You should've seen the look on his face when he got down to the part that asked me about my previous jobs! I'll never forget him telling me, "You're either going to be really good at this, or you're seriously stupid!" Look, after being turned down at 43 places, I had to be better than good. I had to become GREAT, or else I was going to waste more time being disappointed, getting turned down, filling out application after application, while making ZERO dollars doing them. And no, they're not fun to fill out. Especially the funny ones at the grocery stores with the rolling ball that served as a mouse, and a ridiculously gross and dirty keyboard that had some keys that required you to slam down just for them to register a letter. So I took home ALL of the brochures, scared, but excited as all heck, and studied the crap out of them!

So here goes… if you want to become a great salesperson, PLEASE, PLEASE PLEASE LEARN your products. There's nothing worse than buying something from someone who has NO CLUE what he or she is selling, whether it's a phone, a TV, a car, a house, anything. Imagine you wanted the latest borderless flatscreen with the sharpest, most detailed picture, all of the smart internet connectivity technology, and the person at the electronics store had no clue what the difference was between 4K and 1080 meant. Or imagine buying a house from a realtor that had no clue what a sump pump was. I don't even know if they should, but I'm not a realtor… so don't buy a house from me.

However, if you want to buy a vehicle, I'm your guy! Because I took the time to learn my vehicles. All of their features, their advantages, what makes them awesome. It doesn't matter what you sell! If you take the time to REALLY LEARN it, with the mindset to better SERVE your customers and connect them to how your product can benefit them, then you're on the right track! Not only that, this will build tons and tons of confidence for you when they're asking you questions about your product, and the information flows seamlessly off the tip of your tongue.

Secondly, DO NOT LIE! Make sure your word is impeccable. This isn't just a rule for sales. You have to truly fight the urges to compromise in any area of your life. And being a salesperson will definitely challenge you in this over and over again. Think about it. The word salesman is almost always preceded with the word sleazy... so thank goodness for me, I had the fear of God looming over me with choice to live a "free" life, set by truth, or go back to the drug-addicted painful cycles that I pretty much believed was a direct correlation to living a life of lies! Choice A please.

Without even knowing it then, this really set me apart as a car salesman. Now don't get me wrong. I am not some high-almighty, self-righteous, perfect human-being that told the truth 100% of the time. There were times that I compromised. There were times that I hid the whole truth. There were times where I may have fibbed just a little bit. There were A LOT of times that I over exaggerated. There were definitely times where I passed on completely bogus information that I received from someone else. But through every one of those moments and opportunities, I weighed them heavily against my effort to become a truthful, honest person with an impeccable word! And if my actions did not resonate with the truth, I did everything I could to make the RIGHT CHOICE the next time. To tell the complete truth. To calm down on my exaggerations.

To fact-check the relayed-information, especially when a part of me had a gut feeling that it wasn't true.

On a spiritual level, telling a lie creates a wall, a barrier, a disconnect in energy between you and someone else. It's a feeling that may or may not even be understood by the person you're lying to. But that lie is there... and it creates a wedge between you and the person you're lying to. Shoot, it might make you a sale right now... but in one way or another, you will miss out on so many more rewarding factors that will truly make you a successful salesperson.

I become friends with about 90% of my customers... the other 10% of them don't want friends, and that's okay. These are customers that bring me their friends, family members, their kids, co-workers, even strangers. And the best part is, they talk so highly of me and build me up in a way that instantly breaks down all of the sales barriers that a successful salesperson meticulously chips away at when it comes to new customers.

Being an honest, truthful, person is the greatest foundation to making a friend. And what have you heard a thousand times in sales meetings all across the world? Who would you want to buy something awesome from? A friend! Someone you trusted, and truly believed had your best interest in mind. I'm not talking about one of your friends who just started working for another multi-level marketing company, has no clue what they're doing, and is badgering you to buy their products or join their team. I'm talking about a friend who is at the top of their game, who truly cares about you, and I can't say it enough… someone you TRUSTED! That type of energy and flow does NOT happen if you continuously choose to lie to your customers, the people around you, your family… any one! So if you can help it, do your best to choose telling the truth. Even if you know it might become an objection, a challenge, a problem. Face them head on, and face them truthfully. That way, you and your customer can navigate through the issues together. Unless you're a blood sucking spider, you can't navigate through a web of lies. It's impossible for a liar to get a clear understanding of the situation and head towards and an amazing outcome.

So no, I was not BORN a salesman. But these two foundations of 1. really learning and getting to know my product and 2. choosing not to lie and being as much as I could, a truthful, honest person, set the stage for me to become a great one!

PRACTICAL APPLICATIONS

Take the time to study your products. Get your hands on whatever information you can. Read the brochures, do any of the training courses your company provides. After you're done with those, tap into the all mighty inter-webs and ask Google for more information. You'll be able to gather so much information both from the company side to the consumer side. Be careful of all of the negativity that's out there too. Understand that no single product will ever please EVERY ONE, so take in all of the exciting, positive information about your product and share those tidbits.

Fight any and all temptations to lie. Do not try to justify them. This will shape you into an amazing, trustable sales-person, and an overall, great human being. Lies build the walls that separate us from freely connecting with others, it does not help us to navigate around them.

CHAPTER 2
LEARN FROM THE BEST!

When I first started, I had no idea what I was doing. But neither did the two other newbies they just hired. But since they were the newbies, they were the ones I spent the first few weeks comfortably talking to. We would come into work, do some of the basic training courses, grab lunch for everyone else, run remedial errands, get coffees, fill up cars with gas, and basically, waste a lot of time bullshitting while waiting for a possible opportunity to walk onto the lot. Between my fear of the customers, and all of the other hungry salesmen that worked there, my opportunities were few and far in between. If it wasn't for the management yelling at me for being lazy, I probably would've never taken a fresh "up." That's what they call a new customer that comes onto the dealership without an appointment. My first few ups were horribly botched up. I would constantly run back and forth from the customer to the management asking what to do next. You can only imagine how horrible of an experience that was for them. Thank goodness for "turns." A turn is where we run as fast as we can to the managers so they can send in one of the big guns to come and rescue us from our bumbling selves. As soon as they stepped in, all we had to do was shut our mouths, and watch the magic happen!

Wait! Wow! What a concept. So you're telling me that I can take the risk of grabbing the next opportunity, try my best and possibly make a complete fool of myself, pushing the sale process as far as I can, and when I can't get any further, a knowledgable, smooth talking, sales veteran will do the rest for me and I make HALF the commission??? I'm in!!!! Let's GO!!! For my first three to four months in the business, I think every single one of my deals were SPLIT deals. I would scream, "mine!" for the customers that would drive on the lot, run out the door, greet them with a huge smile, and take it as far as I could go. Then, when I couldn't go any further… I would call in the reinforcements, and the Apache Helicopter would come swooping in to shoot down all of the obstacles that customers threw at me! Wow! Some of the things these veterans would say. Some of the things they would do. Look, I do not condone everything that they did and said, but the things I did resonate with, I tucked into my utility belt for future use.

Listen, if you want to get good at something, one of the fastest ways is by surrounding yourself with people that are the BEST at what you want to get better at! It might be intimidating to approach them, but I promise you this, any one that's really great at what they do, LOVES TALKING ABOUT IT! So ask them questions, listen wholeheartedly, and instead of argue with what you don't agree with, simply take the pieces that connects with you. That does not mean you discard the other things. Not at all. There's probably going to be a lot of things that they tell you that you won't connect with, some of which might make you want to throw up even. If you did, then you'd already BE the best. Unless you know it's morally wrong, TRY THEM… and not just once. Try them over and over again. You're obviously not going to be a master at these techniques the first time you attempt them. And yes, some of them may seem RIDICULOUS, and so out of your personality that it does not make any sense. Still TRY them.

For example, one of the techniques I learned that in the beginning I thought was so ridiculous was the "who got who question." This is where you're test driving in the backseat with a couple riding up front, either married or in a relationship, and you tap one of them on the shoulder and ask, "So who got who?" At first, I felt very awkward asking… but after finally trying it, I got some of the most amazing, heart felt, sometimes funny responses. Especially when they didn't agree on who got who… or if they grabbed each other's hand reminiscing about their first dates… it really broke the ice and allowed me to connect with my customers on a deeper level.

Now I'm not telling you to keep all of them… but the more techniques you try that have been working for the greats, the more opportunities you have at becoming the very best! You'll start keeping the ones that work really well for you in your tool box, and begin effortlessly using them to take amazing care of your customers.

I'll never forget Bill Edmonds. Rest in peace to one of my first mentors in the car biz. From what I could see, he was the "man" at Denver Isuzu Suzuki. He sold the most cars EVERY SINGLE MONTH, and was the person I wanted to beat and surpass. As far as I can remember, I feel like he closed every single deal I ever needed his help on. I may or may not have idolized him a bit even though he was like an overweight, elderly, balding version of superman to me. A Superman with a bad hip. But he sure helped me make good money. The best part was, I was getting to learn all of his methods. The things that he would say to customers when they would object to something. The jokes that he would perfectly throw in to break the ice, and man, he was funny. He told me, "Every laugh you get is worth a thousand dollars. So if you are selling a sixteen thousand dollar car, make them laugh at least sixteen times!" I didn't really understand it then, but I was like, hmmm... that makes sense... right? I didn't yet realize how much of the sales process really dealt with CONNECTING with the other person. Yes, there are hundreds of books on how to manipulate your customers, use their lizard brains against them, and position yourself to close a deal with the right wording, but if you're *really* connecting with your customers, you don't need to resort to manipulative tactics. Can they help your closing percentages? Yes. Definitely. I've read the books, studied them, and used them. They work. But so does connecting with your customers at a deeper level. And between the two, connecting works way better!

And then there was Brett Marshall. He didn't sell the most cars. But he sure made A LOT MORE MONEY than Bill Edmonds did. He was sharp. Dressed to kill with decorated cowboy boots, a matching leather belt, slicked-back-hair, and was so good at convincing people to pay so much more for the same car than anyone else could in the dealership. Yes folks, he was high-grossing customers even on the NEW CARS, not just the used ones with all the markup! In most places, and especially so at a Suzuki dealership, most of the money was made selling the pre-owned vehicles since there was hardly any money to be made on the new cars. So yes, I gravitated to him too. Why the heck not? But I wanted to sell the most cars, AND make the most money. Wouldn't you?

It took about seven months of trials, errors, and turns before it really started clicking for me. I was learning a lot of new things… not just about the cars, but how to sell them… and about people, and how to sell them, too. Unfortunately, I never had the opportunity to beat Bill Edmonds. He retired a couple months before I became somewhat of a sales professional.

However, when he left, they hired a guy named Milt Can-cannon. Oh man. Talk about the poster child for a Used Car Guy! A slick talking, bi-lingual, Italiano / Cubano killer who spoke both Spanish and English with gelled up curly hair that literally crushed the competition. Not just in the amount of sales, but ALSO in the amount of gross he was making per vehicle. I had a new target. But with the way he did things, and how cocky he was, I didn't necessarily want to be him, I wanted to beat him, badly! For the next few months I came close... there were even months where I would be beating him by a few units, up until the last two days, where he would catch up and beat me by a single measly stinking last minute deal!!!! I'll never forget it. It was December of 2007. He had been the reigning champ for the past few months, and he started December off by telling me that there was no way I would beat him before the year was over. At this point, I had been selling cars for a little over a year, learned a heck of a whole lot, and was dying to get my name on a plaque for the number one salesman of the month. And there was no way that anyone was going to stop me! The last day of December 2007 was a snowy one. We were neck and neck. He sold a car, I sold a car. He sold another one, so did I. We were tied. But I wasn't done. And I didn't want to end it off with a tie. I sold another three cars that day and ended up selling FIVE in one day... selling the most I've ever sold in a day, and finally beating the best!

PRACTICAL APPLICATIONS

Find out who the most successful person in your company is. Talk to them, ask them questions. Hang out with THEM and learn as much as you possibly can. Take in as much or as little as they're willing to teach. Note: Most super successful people love talking about their success and are willing to share how they achieve their success. At the same time, stay away from the negativity talk. It's really, really easy to fall into this trap and to sit around and whine about your shit while you're listening to them complain about theirs. Nothing good comes out of this. So surround yourself with the successful and treat the negativity like a plague! Watch how quickly you will improve!

CHAPTER 3
FROM HERO TO ZERO

As I'm writing this chapter, please note that I DID NOT master how to manage the roller coaster a year into the car business. I didn't master this FIVE years in… or seven, eight, or even nine! I learned this at year eleven… and didn't master it till about now, 13 years in, as I'm writing this book. My hope is that I can share all of the awesome things I learned in the past 13 years so you don't have to go through all of the maddening thought patterns that could literally destroy your opportunity for an amazing, wonderful career in sales.

After my big win in December of 2007, I sold a measly 8 cars in the month of January. Note. I sold FIVE in the last day of December, and for the WHOLE month of January, I only sold eight. I went from Hero to Zero in a matter of a day, and I was not ready for the games that it played with my mind. That's what happens every month, when the slate is cleaned, and every one goes back to zero! It may be different time frames for different industries. Some may start over every quarter, others half a year, or yearly. But regardless of which time frame you're working on, you start back at zero! At least that's what it feels like. And the quotas that need to be met, goals that need to be hit, and records that need to be broken, start from zero all over again!

And that would be fine, if we weren't shaped into believing so many lies that have been engrained into our society. "Survival of the fittest," "Kill or be killed," "Winners and losers," and "the Coffee is for closers only!" The truth is, we live in a world of abundance. Yet, when it comes to sales and making money, so many of us feel like if someone else got the customer and the deal, we missed out. Especially if they ended up grabbing the BIG deal that made a LOT of money, as if that was the last good paying customer on the planet. I struggled with this for years! Instead of getting my butt ready for the next customer to come on the lot, I would focus on how horrible it was that I missed the last opportunity. As if *that* one was the only one that was going to be a deal… I would beat myself up for going to the bathroom or eating lunch at the worst time possible, and not being there for the customer. It messed me up so bad that when the next customer *DID* come on the lot, I'd be stuck inside my head, instead of focusing on taking such amazing care of the person I had in front of me. Asking them the right questions and actually listening and *HEAR*ing what they're saying so I can best serve them.

You KNOW the difference when you're on! Cause when you're feeling good, and you're on, you feel like nothing can stop you! You have the energy to do all the sales steps that would otherwise feel like extra, tedious, unnecessary work. Note. These are the steps that you SHOULD BE DOING every single time any way. Again, asking the right questions. Listening. Getting to really know your customer, finding out what problems they have that you can solve, and building rapport. And when you begin to do this really well, you actually cross over to a place that some people call the "zone."

For so long, I tried to figure out how to get "in the zone," and how to keep myself from falling out of it. But as long as I let OUTSIDE factors affect me, I was on a constant roller coaster. If I was doing well and I was the only one selling car after car, crushing the competition, I was in the zone. But as soon as someone else speared the big whale, my freight train going full speed ahead would get derailed. As I sit and write this now, I look back, shaking my head, thinking about the hundreds of hours that I wasted, worrying about someone else... how many deals they were doing, how much money they were making, only to realize the thousands of opportunities I actually missed in the wake of it. I can't even imagine trying to calculate the amount of dollars that that equates to, I'm done throwing away precious moments.

Thank goodness I now have the choice to look back with a different set of lenses called gratitude. These are the lenses that I could have and definitely SHOULD HAVE used way back when. Funny thing is, gratitude is probably the greatest weapon against depression, the ups and downs of the roller coaster, the feelings of lack, and the madness of competition. If I step away from what's going on… all the deals happening around me while I can't seem to catch a break, being down two to three car deals from my competition, managers spoon feeding another salesman a deal… whatever the circumstances. If I redirect my focus to gratitude and appreciation, I can literally shift my energy, and set myself up to get back into the zone!

Try this for me.

List 10 things that you are grateful for. Yes yes, I know that you might've heard or done this before. You've probably listed out even more than ten things and still felt like crap. Maybe you're someone who feels as though they don't even have much to be grateful for at all! Maybe you're drowning in so much debt, can barely afford your car payment, or maybe you don't even have a car. You could be someone getting evicted from your apartment right now. Regardless what your situation is, there are still things you can be grateful for. But instead of simply listing those things out one after another, let's dig really deeply into each one of them and reach a level of gratitude that you can actually feel. Doing this changed my life.

Let me give you an example of how deep it can go. I am so grateful for my cool memory foam, Tempur-Pedic Mattress, 1000 thread count sheets, my fluffy down comforter, duvet cover, and two king sized down pillows, on top of the additional two queen sized Temperpedic memory foam pillows that I tuck in between my knees. I am so grateful that I get to wake up energized from such a wonderful, comfortable, decked out bed that I practically melt in every night. Then I pause for a moment and take it in a little deeper and think, I'm so grateful I even have a bed to sleep on. A bed that's in a home with four walls. With an HVAC system that keeps the temperature of my home cool in the summer, and more importantly, warm in the blistering cold winters. And then my heart shifts from focusing on myself, and I think about all of the people who would give their right arms for a comfortable night's sleep in a safe, warm home. People who can't even afford to pay their gas bill and are piling on bundles and bundles of clothes trying to stay warm in theirs. After that, I go even deeper. And I think about all of the people who don't even have a place to come home to. Or a bed to sleep in… or the bundles of clothes to keep them warm in the blistering cold, especially when it's wet and raining, like it is right now as I'm writing this. And bundles? Some of them don't even have a shirt on their back! No lie, some times, I cry. And at that point, I reach a level of gratefulness that breaks me.

The thing is, it doesn't matter how much or how little we have. We can do this with anything and everything we are grateful for. It could be something as large as a 10,000 square foot mansion or as little as a warm, home cooked meal. If we do the practice of digging deeper into it, we can reach a level of gratefulness that can help us tap into a different frequency that guides us back into the zone a heck of a lot quicker than sitting around, waiting for something good to happen TO us. Our level of joy isn't dependent on how much we have, rather, it's how much we appreciate it.

PRATICAL APPLICATIONS

So focus on the good things in your business. Celebrate the victories. Celebrate them big. Even the small victories. Take the time to point out all the good things that are happening. And if it's just one good thing, dig deeper into that one, good thing. Aligning yourself in the frequency of being grateful shifts your energy into receiving so much more. We truly do live in a world of abundance. However, it's **our belief of limitations** that prevents us from being able to receive all that this world has to offer.

CHAPTER 4
EAT SHIT FOR TWO YEARS

During my first year at Denver Suzuki, I practically LIVED at the dealership... not because I all of a sudden went from being a hardcore meth addict to a full blown workaholic... but more so because I wasn't allowed in Raul's house when he wasn't home. I lived in his basement, but he had a wife and five kids to protect. Not that I would've ever hurt them, but how was he supposed to know that? So when Raul was out the door to work, so was I. Plus, I didn't have a car yet, and he was my only ride. Now here's how it worked. The car business has early shifts, late shifts, all-day-long shifts, and every employee worked every one of them, depending on the day. For me, the early shift days were so much easier. Raul would drive me to work before heading off to his, which meant I'd be the first one there, then he would come pick me up when he was done, just in time for a wonderful, home cooked meal prepared by his wife, Jennie. The tough part was my late shift days. I'd be scheduled to work from 1pm to 9pm which is only an eight hour shift. However, since I wasn't allowed in Raul's house when he wasn't home, I was the first one there at 7:45 am, and I'd be there all the way till 9pm. The dealership didn't even open till 8:30! And this lasted for about a year. Following the regular schedule of two early shifts, two late shifts, and one open to close shift was tough enough… but my weeks consisted of two early shifts, and a whole rest of the week full of open to close days! Even my day OFF was a day that I was at work. If it weren't for the fact that I applied to 43 different places and this was the only place that hired me, I would've quit a loooooong time ago and looked for something else. But this was ALL THAT I HAD, and thank goodness for that, because the first year of working my butt off set me up for success!

Gary Veynerchuck said it best! "Eat shit for two years, and eat caviar for the rest of your life!" Now I'm not much for caviar, but I sure do love the fact that I can eat $70 steaks whenever the heck I feel like it… and take family and friends and treat them to the amazing experience too! I busted my butt for those first two years, and with Raul's help, was able to make smarter financial decisions, and establish disciplines that have put me in the position where I haven't had to worry about money for the past 11 years.

Regardless what profession you go into, if you give it your undivided attention, learn as much as you can from the people who are extremely successful at it, read the coinciding books, put in the work, and decide then and there that you will not quit ever, you will achieve greatness. Seriously. But here's the thing. Eating shit for two years doesn't *just* mean that you have to work hard and grind it out for seven hundred thirty days. It also means that you've gotta make a lot of sacrifices and establish disciplines that will help you *stay* successful.

One of the greater techniques I learned was financial budgeting. Working on a commission-only job, you have to make sure you save enough money to survive slow months. There's nothing worse than being a broke, desperate salesman. Sure, you may be hungry to work hard, and go out there and grind your butt off to feed your family or pay your rent, but that desperation rubs off on your customers, and the translation doesn't go well. It may be a great driving force the first few times around, but if you are habitually broke due to bad habits, irresponsible spending, and a limited mindset, your sales career is headed towards years of stress and tons of turbulence. You'll have gray hairs by the time you're thirty. And if you happen to be one of the thirty year old salesmen with gray hairs reading this book, I pray you find something in here that will help you find peace and enjoyment for the rest of your career.

Listen, SAVE AS MUCH MONEY AS YOU POSSIBLY CAN! I understand that you have utility bills, debt, a car payment, phone, rent, etc. and you've gotta make sure to pay those on time! But when it comes to whether or not you should go out this weekend and blow all your dough on getting hammered, take it down. Seriously. If you don't take the time to build this discipline, save, and make sacrificial decisions, you will struggle with money for the rest of your life, and your sales career will suffer drastically. You will always be under pressure to sell sell sell, instead of enjoying the heck out of your job, serving and taking care of your customers while making a lot of money. There's a huge difference. It's about denying yourself from immediate gratification for that longer lasting, real, satisfaction. I may have went a bit extreme, but here's how I did it. I signed up to have Denver Suzuki do a direct deposit to my US Bank checking account. That way, I wouldn't have to go and cash it and have a lot of money in my hands that I could easily blow. From there, I paid all of my bills, gave my ten percent to the church, and put the remaining amount, however big or small, in a savings account. I created my own personal three-ten method. Check it out. If I wanted to buy something that I "needed but could live without," for example, brand new work clothes, work shoes, the fancy hair gel, Dove Soap, I would need to have three times the amount that it cost in my savings account. That wasn't too tough to do. But here's the thing. If I wanted to buy something that I simply "wanted," or spend the money to go out to a movie, I would have to have TEN TIMES the amount that it cost in my account. A night out to the movies cost about twenty bucks. That means I would have to have a minimum of $200 sitting in my savings account just to justify going. A lot of people thought that was crazy… but after two years of suffering through it, I haven't had to check to see if there was enough money in my account to buy something

I needed or *wanted*. There was more than enough. And there has *been* more than enough ever since.

PRACTICAL APPLICATIONS

Work hard. And do more than your job expects of you. Work more hours than you're scheduled to work. Become extremely valuable to your company by the amount of effort you're willing to put in. People that argue how they are not paid enough to do some extra work, or say that's not what my job entails, rarely ever excel past their position. Now, if you're going to do this, but you're complaining the whole time, you're better off NOT doing it. Or if you're planning on doing this so you can boast about how many hours you work and how you do this and that, then just don't do it. It'll backfire on you. Work hard, be humble… but have fun with it! Share your excitements, be enthusiastic, and curb your complaints.

Also, open up a checking and savings account and establish a budgeting method that works for you! There are hundreds of books out there, a bunch of amazing apps, and people that can help you put one together. Note, YOU are your biggest money issue. Not how much you make, and not how big your bills are. It's YOU. So if you can learn how to handle YOU when it comes to money now, then you can live the rest of your life not having to **worry** about it.

CHAPTER 5
BEING NUMBER ONE!

Do you want to be the number one salesman in your organization?!?!? If you're a go-getter and a high performer, of course you do! We live in a society that glorifies the BEST of the BEST! They're the ones that get all the attention, become celebrity, and get paid a heck of a lot more than the rest, right? Whether you want the bragging rights, or the additional bonus checks for being the top guy, there's a bunch of perks that come along with being the number one, numero uno, head of the pack.

However, the road to greatness does not come without a cost. Some of the costs are worth it, while others are not. After busting my butt for the first two years trying to get there, I've been the number one salesman at my dealership for over nine years and at one point, I was the number one salesman for Suzuki USA in the western region, and number four in the whole nation. And for a small-family owned dealership who wasn't involved in doing any fleet deals and huge numbers, that was a big deal. I consistently outsold everyone in my dealership month in and month out, and the only times I lost my first place position was when I spent two weeks of the month on vacation. I won first place so many times that they actually took me out of the running to compete. Instead, I was the only salesman (outside of the management team) that got a free, all expenses paid demo. Every five thousand miles, I get a brand new, heavily equipped, car or SUV. All maintenance costs paid, car insurance, and no registration costs.

On top of that, going to the regional trainings were a blast for my ego. Being a top salesperson for Suzuki, my name was all over the monthly bulletins and quarterly magazines that Suzuki would send out to the dealerships, which meant that all the other salespeople attending these trainings either heard of me or seen my name on the top list! For the earlier part of my career, this added a lot of fuel to my fire, and helped in keeping me driven. But after the novelty of that wore off, it became an empty void that needed constant filling. And that's when I realized that it was more of a vain pursuit that had kept me trapped in the rat race.

I would miss important events in my family's and my friends' lives from always working. There were times where I felt like I was "missing out" on deals every time I wasn't at the dealership... and I would constantly call and check in to see if we were busy at work during my days off. Even on vacation,

I would constantly log on to our CRM to check emails, make phone calls, and try to make deals happen, rarely being present when I was spending time with my family and friends. During the first year of dating my wife, Jamie, I would constantly check my phone… during dinners, nights dancing, even during the MOVIES!!! Yep, I would step out of the theater to make deals. And check this out. On her birthday, during the second month of us dating, I took her to Alaska! Yes… doing well in the car business affords you the luxury of being able to take your dates to Alaska and fully pay for the vacation without blinking an eye, but even then, during our vacation, I spent so much of it WORKING!!! Looking back, that was madness. There were so many moments I missed out on. And for what? The same cycles of the same contest, on the same spinning hamster wheel month in and month out? These are the parts of the car business (or most of the sales jobs out there) that can wear you out, give you the gray hairs by age thirty, and lead you down the bitter road of hating the job that pays you so well. And that's IF you're winning a lot. Can you imagine how much worse it is when you're not on top? When you're one of the many on a sales force, and your value is only as much as you're selling?

That's what tends to happen when your focus is solely on being the best. Being number one. Beating everyone else. You're either going to find a way to keep staying on top or end up finding yourself in this supposedly cozy little spot of simply being mediocre and settling for it, embittered by the whole sales profession. Either way, you're going to get burnt out. It's inevitable. And after nine years of being on top, that's exactly what happened to me! The mental ups and downs of *being* the best — got the best of me. The thousands of hours I spent at the dealership got to me. All of the awesome events that I missed out on got to me. Even the people I worked with and worked for got to me. So much so that I began looking for a way out. The money I was making was suddenly not enough money for what I was having to put up with. At that point, I was looking for a way out. For something different. An escape!

I started interviewing friends, customers, acquaintances… asking them about what they did, and boldly asking them how much they were making. A select few of my friends were realtors, and with the booming real estate economy in Colorado, they were making A LOT of money. I'm talking so much more money than I was making. Pair that with the feeling of being drained, and I was the perfect candidate to jump ship at any second. I came into work, barely motivated, hating every moment of being stuck at the dealership, thinking about everything else BUT my job… Also, I would go into sales slumps and blame everything from bad leads, a slow month, cemetery Tuesdays, to ridiculous customers. I would come into work irate, short tempered, and argue with my managers about anything and everything. It's a snowball effect. Not only was I an egotistical salesman who felt like he was the best thing since slice bread for the dealership, but I wasn't producing the numbers that I normally did. I mean, how could I? My focus was nowhere near where it needed to be. And if you want to succeed in this business, you've gotta have your head, AND your heart, in the right place. If not, you're wasting your time, your managers' time, and most importantly, your customers' time.

All it took was a very small, insignificant fight with my General Sales Manager Ted Vaughan for everything to implode. It ended off with a quick yelling match and me finally deciding to call it quits. After 11 years of what felt like the same thing over and over again, I was done. Plus, I had a bunch of other reasons that justified me taking the jump. One. I was an aspiring musician and rapping lyricist, and I had saved up more than enough money to give that a real go! Two, I was no longer excited about the car business, and being number one again and again became a worthless victory. It wasn't even a challenge any more, and for the first time, staying in the car business felt like I was stuck in the mud. I had come to a place where I was no longer growing. In all honestly, me leaving was the BEST THING that could've ever happened for the dealership, for me and my family, and most importantly, for every one of my future customers.

Some of the best things in my life happened during the year I took off from the car business, the most important and life changing one being the birth of my first child and only daughter, Araya. I was able to be fully present and there for both my wife and my baby during the ups and downs of the pregnancy, the crazy first weeks of Araya being born, to the amazing months that followed, as a strong, powerful, loving support! I was able to paint Araya's nursery and spend hours putting together her crib and dresser without simply paying someone else to do it for me. On top of that, I made an awesome comeback to making music and doing live performances. In less than a year, I went from performing in small dive bars in front of tiny little crowds with less than fifty half interested people to doing the Half time show for Sparta Combat League's AVM9 Event at the Pepsi Center in front of thousands! I opened up for legendary emcees like Masta Ace, filmed a Grindmode cypher video with him that went viral, and teamed up with an amazing hip hop group called Universal Language Entertainment, packing venues like Cervantes and performing at Arise, as well as collaborating with Dave Connolly and rapping at the Fourth of July Festival in Westminster! During this year, I was able to take a step back away from the madness and really figure out what things were important to me, and ultimately, what truly mattered the most. This gave me a brand new perspective in life, one that I was able to bring with me back to the car business, that changed everything.

First of all, even the concept of coming back to the car business itself was extremely humbling. Like any talented musician, I thought I was going to make it big and never have to come back to work. But after my wife spent three months on maternity leave with our beautiful daughter and then having to go back to work, she realized that the amount of hours she used to put into her job and managing a highly successful dermatology center was no longer her number one priority, Araya was. And I was going to support that, even if it meant coming back to work.

Secondly, a young, hungry salesman by the name of Ryan Oldham started working at my dealership two months after I left, and had begun beating my numbers! Justin, the new car manager, used to call me up on the phone and tell me he beat my numbers, goading me to come back. And I remember telling him, "I'm never coming back. I'm gonna make it big!" So this turn of events was not only humbling, but I was about to face a new challenge in coming back. A salesman at my dealership that was supposedly better than me!

However, Ernest Hemingway said something that made a huge impact in my life. "There is nothing noble in being superior to your fellow men. True nobility lies in being superior to your former self." This wasn't a cop out for me now that someone had already beat my numbers. This was more of a new paradigm that I was going to live by if I was going to make a difference in the way I felt about the car business, sales, and life in general. I was done focusing on competing. The only thing I wanted to beat was the old version of me. So whether that was improving my attitudes, my emotions, my physical fitness, the way I treated people, or how I was going to continue in sales, I was going to focus on improving myself by beating my old self, and not by comparing myself to others or by trying to best them. I have enough of a challenge having to face my own shit. Now to be honest, that was a heck of a lot easier said than done!

I came back in the middle of September, 2018, and Jeff Baca, the owner of the dealership, offered me a $1,000 bonus on top of all of the commissions and spiffs if I hit ten sales in the last two weeks. I knew I could easily do it, although a few people around me had their doubts. I mean, I've been gone about a year. Did I even know how to do the paperwork any more? Needless to say, I hit it. But I did it in only seven days, and that was exciting! But then again, anything that feels new… or "new again," usually is, right? The real question was, "Can I keep it exciting?" Or was I going to fall back into the same cycles I found myself trapped in before I left?

This is where everything changed!

Instead of falling back into the cycles that I used to fall into, I started creating new habits that consistently work. That also meant breaking the bad habits that I had, like constantly checking the sales log. I stopped paying attention to how many deals everyone else was doing. I never realized how much seeing another salesman making deals on a day to day basis affected me. If I came in on a late shift and saw Ryan with two deals already slotted on the board, it would hit me hard. I would start playing different scenarios in my head like did the managers spoon-feed him those deals? What if I had come in earlier, would I have gotten those customers? After 12 years of doing this, thank goodness I became a little bit more aware about my inner emotions, my energy, and how it would affect me, the customers I'd talk to, and my ability to serve them. Knowing that, I had to make the change and stop competing against the other sales people.

Instead, I would focus on beating myself. Yes, deep down I wanted to beat Ryan's record. The one that shattered mine... but I kept it as an underlying, healthy motivator, as opposed to something that I would allow to take over me. Instead of focusing on that, I wanted to focus on taking such great care of my customers, and finding better ways to do it. Not only that, there's a saying in the car business that says, "The best time to sell a car is right after you just sold one." Your energy is high, your excitement is up, and that translates so powerfully to your customers... so does the opposite. So why not shift my perspective and truly be happy FOR Ryan whenever HE makes a deal? Like really be happy for him... I'm already crazy grateful for everything I have, why not be happy for someone else for once. And that was another amazing mind shift that happened, and every time Ryan sold a car, I would end up selling one too.

Look, you've got moment by moment choices that you need to solidify. In other words, you can't allow what happens around you to influence your actions and decisions or allow them to define you. If you do, you'll be living on an up and down roller coaster all of your life. Instead, decide once and for all and continue to make better, empowering, healthy, loving choices *regardless* of your circumstances, and watch THOSE influential actions DEFINE what happens AROUND you! This is where the magic unfolds.

By the way, it took me five months of being back in the car business to crush my all time record, and beat Ryan's record by more than four deals, and it happened on the shortest selling month of the year, February.

PRACTICAL APPLICATIONS

Stop focusing on what every one else around you is doing, focus on yourself. Don't waste your energy trying to BEAT them, rather, focus on beating your own personal achievements… and instead of trying to compete with your fellow salespeople, start lifting each other up. Be quick to help them, even if they're not quick to do the same. Be happy for them when they make deals, even if they're jealous of you.

The effort and awareness that it will take to practice these strategies will help you grow in more ways than you can imagine. Not only that, it will help you maintain the higher frequency that it takes to better connect with your customers.

CHAPTER 6
TAKE ADVANTAGE

Now I don't remember the year this happened, but I will never forget the impact it had on me. While working at Denver Suzuki, a few of the sales staff were ***forced*** to go to a Chip Thomas Sales Training event and I was one of the supposedly unfortunate few selected. All of the other seasoned veterans at the dealership acted like there was nothing more they needed to learn and that these events were a complete waste of time, so I wasn't too excited about going. Plus, I felt like I'd be missing out on a lot of opportunities that would come on the lot that day... but boy was I wrong. The things that I learned from that training, and the processes that I've been able to develop from it has increased my sales opportunities exponentially. If your dealership is offering to pay for these external training events, JUMP AT THE OPPORTUNITY TO GO! You might miss a deal or two that comes in that day, but you'll gain it back a thousand times over in the future, promise!

For me, that seminar pretty much changed the trajectory of my sales career, and I'm hoping I can help skyrocket the trajectory of yours by passing along some of the amazing information I've learned through the years. Instead of being one of the guys that would have to rely solely on floor traffic, economic booms and busts, good days and bad days, the dealership's advertising budget, or running to get the lucky ups, his training seminar taught me how to cultivate a deeper relationship with my clients that would end up bringing me TONS of repeat and referral business for years to come. The best part was, he wasn't just teaching me conceptual ideas, he was actually doing them as a car salesman himself, and thriving abundantly from it!

Chip Thomas taught me the value of taking pictures with each and every one of my customers. We both used a disposable camera that I would get double developed. I'd keep one copy in a photo album on my desk at work, and send the other one to the customer. Now, with the advent of the digital cameras on our phones, I am able to take 4–5 pictures, text it to them, post it online, and tag them for them to share with their friends.

The point was to make the event special! They're spending a lot of money with me to buy their vehicle, let's make it special! On top of that, I get to save their contact information in my phone with a picture of them so that I never forget them!!!! How awesome do you think they feel when they call, and

I address them by their name, knowing exactly who it is and the exact vehicle they bought from me???

Moreover, the Chip Thomas seminar also taught me the importance of sending out personalized thank you cards… instead of just sending out the generic thank you c ards, I take the time to create an amazing, artistic design, and hand write a specific thank you that talks about our experience, again, making sure that the customers felt special.

Chip even taught me about making sure to call every one of my customers on their birthdays. I know most of the CRM's send out automatic birthday emails for you, but those SUCK! If they're your customers, CALL THEM PERSONALLY, or TEXT THEM PERSONALLY… there's a huge difference between that and an automatic, generic email. Remember, the point is to let them know how special they are… and there's nothing special about generic.

The thing is, these should be part of your basic fundamentals. The sales process shouldn't only be about mastering the steps to making a sale, they should also weigh heavily on the work it takes to maintain the relationships with customers you've already done business with. This is your gold mine. And I can't stress this enough… You need to take care of your gold mine… Mass emails with specials and deals do not count when it comes to follow up. That's just annoying. And although sending out monthly or quarterly newsletters with amazing, relevant content is great, it isn't mining your gold.

Take the time to continue touching base with your customers. Pick up the phone and just let them know you're still thinking about them!

PRACTICAL APPLICATIONS

Go to training seminars. Take online courses. Read books. Start implementing the things you learn from them. Keep the ones that work best!

CHAPTER 7

BUT THAT WAS CHIP, THIS IS ME, WHO ARE YOU?

So WHO are you? What makes you different from anyone else? Why should *I* buy from **YOU???** Also, take an honest look in the mirror and ask yourself, would YOU want to buy from YOU??? If the answer is a blatant "No," then you probably shouldn't be selling anything because you might be a tad bit shady… or maybe even a downright crook. But look, if you *would* buy from you, then what are the reasons WHY you would buy something from you???

For me, I can easily rattle off why any of you should buy from me. But these reasons didn't come to me in one day. These came from years of development, and the reasons continue to grow from this point, as I discover new ones and am continuously evolving the older ones.

Reason Number One: I truly believe that no other car salesperson will treat you better than I can. I don't just say this. I know this and I do this.

Reason Number Two: I give EVERY SINGLE CUS-TOMER my direct cell phone number and save THEIR number AND picture in my phone so that I can do my best to remember every single one of them... not only that, I save the vehicle they purchased in my phone, so when any one of my customers call, I know exactly who it is, what vehicle they purchased, and answer the call with their name instead of, "hello? Who is this again? What car did you buy?"

Reason Number Three: I become friends with 90% of my customers. The other 10% of them don't want friends, and that's okay with me. If they're open to it, I also add them on Facebook or connect with them through Instagram and keep up with them and their families. Look, not everyone is comfortable with you adding them on social media, so MAKE SURE to ask them.

Reason Number Four: I don't hide away from problems. I run towards them and do everything I possibly can to help out, even if it means having to come out of my own pocket to do so! I'll never forget the first time I had to do this. I had given the wrong information to a customer about a vehicle I sold and after he bought it and had it inspected, it needed brakes. Through miscommunication and my misunderstanding, I had thought that we already replaced those brakes, and I TOLD HIM that... but I was wrong. My dealership shouldn't pay for my mistake, and neither should my customer. After quite a bit of internal grumbling and personal struggle, I offered to make it right and cough up the dough. The whole fix cost me about $200 out of pocket. However, what I didn't realize was the amazing windfall that comes from truly doing the right thing. He sent me FOUR CUSTOMERS in the next few weeks that netted me over 3 grand to my pocket! It was one of those lessons and blessings that taught me to always run TOWARDS problems. If you do anything to try and help them, you end up gaining a customer for life!

Reason Number Five: I don't send out AUTOMATIC BIRTHDAY WISHES. My CRM does. But I follow it up with a personal text and / or phone call. I personally don't like the canned birthday wishes and will never reply to one via email. However, a quick personal text is great, and can even spark up an awesome conversation.

Reason Number Six: I take pictures with each and every single one of my customers. (unless of course they truly object. I won't force anyone to do so if they don't want to) However, I let them know that it is the best way for me to remember who they are. With as many cars as I sell, and all of the customers that I meet, it's very difficult to remember every one of them without a face to go with it.

These reasons have earned me the title "Most Loved Car Salesman," from quite a few of my customers. The title really resonated with me... I knew it was perfect for what I was doing and trying to achieve, so I took that and ran with it. I also knew that the title would have HUGE shoes for me to fill if I were going to claim that with each and every NEW customer I met. So I had to answer some big questions. Like what would it take to actually BE the most loved car salesman? And after a year intermittently thinking about it, I found the answer. I would have to LOVE my customers the most.

And that's what gave birth to my own personal branding. I redesigned all of my business cards, I changed the signature to all of my emails. I removed the title, "Internet Sales Director," and replaced it with hashtag #MostLovedCarsalesman. I even created a symbol to go with it. It looks like a flame. It signifies the awesome changes and the phoenix like transformations that my life has gone through, and it's also a design of my initials. It's a small b and a capitalized Q. I wanted to make the b small, as a symbol of keeping my personal ego in check, and capitalize the Q to honor my family. I put one of these stickers on every single car I sell, unless a customer explicitly requests that I don't. I've had less than a handful of customers request that, out of the thousands of others that proudly carry my symbol on the backs of their cars.

Surprisingly, I've even had customers who did want ANY-THING on their car, ask me to have the DEALERSHIP branding sticker to be removed, but still wanted mine displayed prominently where everyone could see it. I've also had other customers post pictures of other cars with the bQ sticker on their Facebook pages and tag me, or text them to me, letting me know that they spotted one while they were driving… As flattering as that is, PLEASE DO NOT TAKE PICTURES while driving… and if you must, just do it safely ;)

My brand has now created a standard that I need to continuously live up to. I can't introduce myself as "the most loved car salesman" and act like a jackass right after. Setting up this level of expectation has me giving my all each and every time, providing the very best customer service… the highest level of care, and in my case, the most love.

The best part about all of this is, NONE OF THESE TECHNIQUES WE LEARN FROM THE GREATS ARE COPYRIGHTED, which means, try a bunch that resonate with you then jack the shit out of them. Snatch em up, take them and use them. Master them until they, too, become an amazing part of your basics and fundamentals of doing business, and watch how you thrive in anything that you do. Learn to love ALL of your customers, and I promise they'll love you too!

PRACTICAL APPLICATIONS

So figure out what things you can do that will set you apart from the rest. And once you figure it out, do them all the time. Make it a part of your process. Don't do it for some and not for others… keep it consistent. That way, these processes become a part of you, and every one you interact with will be able to sense it without you having to tell them. And if by chance, you end up discovering completely new, untried methods, don't keep them for yourself, share them. Spend your down time talking about *that* instead of the complaining and shit talk. Build each other up!

CHAPTER 8

LEARN TO LIKE THE PEOPLE YOU WORK WITH

It was noon on a Saturday, our busiest day of the week, late in February, and I was just about to finish off a record breaking month when the owner of my dealership, Jeff Baca, decided to take a deal away from me. Our service writer, Kat, who's seen how I treat all of my customers first hand, wanted me to be the one to take care of her sister since she was looking for a replacement vehicle for the one she just totaled. However, Jeff offered the deal to Mike Larson, a fellow salesman instead. I became infuriated! Not only did Kat ask me specifically so that her sister could get the best care possible, I felt that Jeff would want to do the same and give the guy in the dealership who deserved the deal most, the referral deal. Frantically, I texted him about how mad that just made me and how stupid it was that he was taking this deal away from me. I didn't get a response. That made me even more angry. The worst part was, he was off on Saturdays, preventing me from being able to walk right into his office and hash things out. By Sunday, still no reply. And by this time, the conversations I was having with him (IN MY HEAD) were spiraling out of control. My ego was telling me I DESERVED that deal, and my anger was judging the crap out of him, thinking he was foolish to give the deal to someone else! To make matters worse, Mike Larson and the team were not able to make the deal with Kat's sister. This only fueled my ego even more and clouded my thinking to the point where Monday came, and I decided, "Fine! If Jeff wants to be that way, I will simply choose to ignore him, continue crushing it, and do it whether or not I was in good terms with him." I know that if I had been the one to take care of Kat's sister, it would've easily been a deal where everyone was taken care of. On top of that egotistical mindset, I started getting involved with the gossip and bad talk about the mistakes Jeff was making as an owner, especially during the slow weeks, to the point where I started believing that it was all his fault that everything was going wrong, and why the company culture sucked.

Normally, I come into work, super high energy, saying hi to all of the employees and getting a bunch of people pumped up. (A few thought it a bit overwhelming, but for the rest of them, it was a good pick me up) When Jeff would arrive, I would wait till he settled in, then walk into his office for a little chit chat, usually with something motivating to get myself going. Sometimes we'd plan another lunch to an awesome restaurant in Boulder, other times, we'd talk about the numbers I'd hit this month and possible spiffs, bonuses, and prizes in store. It was great. But since I got no reply from that text, it was done. I would walk by his office as though he didn't even exist. I wasn't going to be the one to back down.

The next two months were some of the worst months I've ever had in the car business. My ego was flared, my heart was closed, and my focus all over the place. Me and Jeff barely said anything to each other these two months and the dealership, as well as my sales numbers, were suffering badly. Yet instead of swallowing my pride and talking to him about it, I got angrier and angrier and withdrew even more. To the point where I started entertaining going somewhere else and starting all over again, as if the grass is actually greener on the other side. Listen guys, unless you're getting abused where you're at, the grass isn't greener on the other side... it's greener wherever you choose to water and nurture it!

The problem is, it's really hard to realize that when you're in the thick of it. Caught in all the drama, the hardest thing for us to see is that the only real problem is us. We get so caught up seeing all of the problems around us, complaining about them, extending the gossip, and wonder why our issues continue to feel like they're getting worse.

It took awhile for me to realize this, but when I finally stopped pointing the finger at everyone and everything else around me, I realized it was my ego that got the best of me.

I was blaming Jeff for TAKING something away from me, when in all truth, Jeff has been nothing but extremely generous to me. And even though this situation may not have felt like that… the truth is, it's waaaaaay bigger than Jeff and me. There's a greater force behind all of this. And in knowing that, we are either in a state of gratitude or a state of complaining. When I started complaining, I took myself out of alignment from being able to make deals easily. Remember in chapter three, when I talked about managing the roller coaster, and getting back in the zone? Well, one of the fastest ways to get OUT of the zone is by complaining. And the fastest way to get back IN the zone is gratitude. But it can't go without a good clearing.

For example. When the weeks started getting worse and worse, I figured I'd brush up on some good self help books, "The Power of Now" by Eckhart Tolle, and a couple of amazing sales books from Grant Cardone to help me get right back in the zone. I even started doing my whole gratitude meditations to put myself back into that frequency. Unfortunately, I was still harboring all of the anger and resentment towards Jeff, and that was the giant wall between me and the zone that I so desperately wanted to get back in.

Look, you can't fake this shit! You can't pretend to be all grateful while holding on to so much discontent with some-one, especially when it's the boss at your job, you know, the job you're desperately trying to self-talk your way back into being in the zone at! It just doesn't work that way. Everything is off. Down to the energy level and the vibe that you're giving off. From your co-workers, to every customer that steps onto your lot. You end up pulling yourself out of being able to serve them, and go back to trying your best to simply SELL them… and that's where the disconnect creates a giant gap between you and where you want to be.

It took awhile for me to finally muster up the courage to walk into the boss's office and tell him I was sorry for my egotistical lash out. He told me that my attitude and brazen texts had undermined him, and he felt really disrespected by them, especially after all of the years that we've known each other and worked together. He felt as though I went from being grateful to an egotistical maniac and quite honestly, he was right. However, my sincere apology put a tiny crack in the giant wall that we've been building in between us for the past two months. Unfortunately, it wasn't enough to break it down yet, and the following week felt just as bad as it had felt for the past two months, maybe worse even. But knowing where I went wrong, I no longer harbored any resentment towards him. It wasn't about HIM any more. It was about me and my inability to respond in the best way I could to a situation that I didn't like.

Unfortunately, I wasn't back to making deals, (at least not in the number of sales that I'm used to, nor with the enjoyable ease that it usually is for me to sell cars) and the thought of leaving and going somewhere else kept creeping in. I had two choices… keep trying to push through, or go into his office and hash it out.

I walked in, closed the door, and simply asked him, have we reached the point where our friendship is unrepairable? That honest, down-to-the-core question was enough to break through all of the bad energy, anger, and any resentment we were left holding onto. It's soooo crazy how everything changes when you finally take ownership of the bullshit that's happening around you and realize well, it's actually YOU! And unless you make the conscious decision to create an elevated action, you will stay in that lower state… for as long as you continue to choose NOT to act. Or to continue blaming someone else, alleviating you from your responsibility and opportunity to fix your mess.

Look, it's rarely ever an easy thing to see this clearly. Most of us spend our lives never looking solely in the mirror and asking ourselves, what could I have done better in this situation. We're too busy blaming everything else. The problem is, most of those things we are blaming are justifiably at fault too, so it makes it even harder to see that WE are the true source of the problem. And the only reason we are experiencing this is because 1. We've either got a lesson to learn from it, or 2. Our thoughts and our actions are bringing it to us.

So if you're feeling like you keep cycling through the same shit over and over again at your dealership or life in general, and you're one of the guys that sit around complaining about everything, gossiping about everyone, and wondering why nothing gets better… it's YOU. Seriously… it's just you.

After that last run with the owner of the dealership, taking two months to apologize for my madness, and another week for the walls to finally break down, I'm happy to report that I'm back in the zone… This time, with another deeper insight of how to respond to future situations that I may disagree with.

Listen, it isn't worth it. Acting out of pride and ego, there's just no win to it. And the cost, geez. Not only did it cost me tons of sales… but it also cost me hours upon hours of happiness that I could've been enjoying. Next time I'm hit with something that might throw me off course, I'll take a step back… focus on gratitude, then respond. 'Cause any time you respond out of gratitude, you've got God and the whole universe backing you, ready to bless you abundantly.

PRACTICAL APPLICATIONS

Communicate. Seriously. Communicate. If you've got something to say, say it. Don't hold anything in. Come from a place of humility and respect, but make sure you talk it out. Keeping it in and having two-way conversations in your own head accomplishes nothing.

The best part about talking it out respectfully means you'll have an opportunity to learn more about the other person. And once we can drop our pride and our own personal judgements, we become open to understanding the other person, and maybe just maybe, liking them even.

CHAPTER 9
CONNECTING AT THE HEART LEVEL

I'll never forget our Friday morning meetings. We've had them EVERY SINGLE Friday for the past 12 years, talking about the same things over and over again. The sales and finance managers would take turns training us during these Friday morning meetings. In the beginning, I learned a lot from them. All of the sales processes and steps involved with making a sale… especially since I was someone who did not know ANYTHING about selling anything. But after awhile, the meetings became boring, hearing the same exact thing over and over again, week in, week out, month in, month out, year in, year out, decade in… and 12 years later, it's still the SAME DAMN MEETING!

The problem I was seeing was that so many sales people would get hired, trained, then fail and quit. Only a very few would actually be able to utilize the training and make a really good living from it. I think I've worked with over 300 sales people who have been hired and left since I started. But what was the problem? I mean, it's a sales job, and the pay plan is simple. The more you sell, the more you make. So what's missing in the sales trainings that are keeping amateur sales people from reaching great numbers? Is it the people we are hiring? That's part of it. But could it be that after 300 people in the past 12 years, that maybe something was missing in the training? Maybe our sales process was missing some few key elements that could actually make it work!

Step One. Meet and Greet. Welcome your customers to your business establishment, introduce yourself with a huge smile and ask for their names. Step Two. Build rapport. Ask them questions about *them* and find common ground. Step Three. Qualify. Find out what they're looking for. What their budget is. What are their needs and wants. Step Four. Presentation. Show them a product that fits what they're looking for, or be a professional and show them things that are similar, that offer them a great option. Step Five. Demonstration. Show them how this product can meet their wants and needs, or more importantly, solve a problem for them. If you're doing car sales, take them on a test drive. Step Six. Trial Close. Call out buying signs. MAKE SURE to ask for the sale! Step Seven. Negotiations. Step Eight. Close the Deal. Step Nine. Deliver the Product. Step Ten. Follow Up. Step Eleven. Follow Up. Step Twelve… FOLLOW UP!

Give or take a few that you can substitute or blend together, these steps are a great foundation to making a sale. And if you learn them well enough, and use them every single time you talk to a customer, you'll probably make a decent living. Statistically, you'll sell 25% of the people you talk to. So the more people you talk to, while following the steps outlined to make a sale, the more sales you make. You just have to end up talking to a WHOLE LOT OF PEOPLE...

I'm not sure about you, but a 75% fail rate has gotta get tiring and depressing. What if the whole sales process and the training behind it needs to get a huge make over? What if instead of training our staff to sell, sell, sell... we can train them to serve, and serve amazingly well... hear me out.

Regardless what you say or don't say to a customer, most of your underlying intentions leak through the smallest motions in your body language, inflections in your voice, and the choice of words that you use. So if you've been trained to sell, sell, sell them, they can feel that. And if they feel that, it will take a lot of work and convincing, closing techniques, discounting prices, manipulation and sometimes, even lying to get them to buy your product. Sure, once in awhile, you'll meet a customer that will WANT your product more than you even want to sell it to them... but those are rare. We call those Lay Downs in the car business because the customer just comes in and lays down their money to buy what ever we choose to sell them. Most of the other customers are just people that have problems that hopefully your product can solve. The best way to find that out is by learning how to serve them as best as you possibly can.

Take a trip with me real quick. Let's just say you had to be completely blunt and honest with every customer that you meet. Could you imagine telling them, hey, thank you for coming in to my dealership. I don't want you to waste my time. I want you to already know what you want, and after talking with me for a bit and using up my time test driving, you better buy something. I want you to pay me full price or more for it so I can make a ton of money clubbing you like a baby seal. That sounds insane, right? But honestly, that's what the majority of the sales people in the car business really feel. It's to the point where if the customer doesn't buy, most of them have the nerve to call them stupid, crazy, or dumb after they leave. Well, who's the dumb one? Truth is, they didn't buy from someone who didn't give a flying fuck about them, who only wanted to take them for all they've got, or force them into a car or product that didn't really meet their needs. Sounds to me like they were actually pretty smart and were intelligent enough to dodge a bullet. Sadly, you're the bullet.

But what if we trained our sales force to truly SERVE our customers. To get to know them. To really find out what their needs are, and what problems we can solve. To stop caring about simply trying to sell them just to make money. Especially if we do not provide a product that solves their problems, or meets their wants and needs. Look, if your focus is solely about making money, not caring about the customers you're taking the money from, you're doing it backwards. But if your focus is to truly serve your customers, then you'll tap into something most sales people never experience. You'll start connecting with all of your customers from a heart level. Suddenly, instead of using manipulation or closing techniques, your intuition will start finding connections on how your product can truly solve their problems. And when you can truly solve their problems, customers will happily pay you what you're worth.

So let's paint the same scenario of having to be completely blunt and honest with every customer you meet. Hi, welcome to Boulder Hyundai. My name is Bernard Quisumbing and I am the most loved car salesman in Colorado. I am here to serve you to the very best of my ability and hopefully provide you with a product that meets your wants and needs, or can solve a problem you have. I will offer it to you at a fair price, and make sure to give you the very best customer service possible. I'll deliver the best service before, during, and after the sale, especially if you have any questions or issues with the product I offer you. If you're not ready to make a decision, I will happily show you the products I have to offer, what they do, and do it as enthusiastically as I can, giving you as much information as you need to make an informed decision. **I definitely want you to buy from me**, but mostly because I know that no one can take care of you as well as I can and will. However, if my product doesn't make sense for you, it was a pleasure meeting you!

Now which person would you rather give your money to? Seriously? The answer becomes very easy to figure out, especially when it's slapped in your face that bluntly. But it's not easy to transition to this higher frequency and emotional state. Most of us are selfish. We want the money and we want it now. Funny thing is, we are the ones getting in the way the most. So what if we changed our training into teaching our staff how to serve enthusiastically, happily, energetically, and sincerely?

Instead of seeing every customer who walks onto our lot as a dollar sign, what if we considered them as an opportunity to meet someone awesome and serve them as best as we can. Let's not gauge success or failure in relation to whether or not it was a sale or no sale. Wait wait wait... before you slam this book shut, HEAR ME OUT! What if we gauge our success based on HOW WELL we served our customers? How enthusiastic were we when we were showing them our product? How often did we make them laugh? How much did we learn about them? How hard did we try to find solutions to their problems? How well did we maintain our attitudes? See, if we keep making improvements to those metrics, the outcomes will skyrocket!!! Step back and really think about it. If your sales force continuously demonstrated their products enthusiastically, made their customers laugh constantly, got to know them, and gave their all trying to find solutions to their problems while maintaining a great attitude through the ups and downs of the process, well, shoot... HOW MANY MORE SALES DO YOU THINK YOUR TEAM WILL MAKE??? A LOT!!!! Your 25% closing ratio will jump to 60–70, maybe even 80%. And sure, you won't sell ALL OF THEM, but at least you'll be a hell of a lot happier of a person serving your customers from the bottom of your heart. And I can tell you from personal experience, a 30% failure rate isn't tiring OR depressing... because a 70% success rate where 99% of your customers are realllllly happy, appreciate the crap out of you, send you their friends and family, and end up becoming your friends, is such a freaking awesome thing! Suddenly, work isn't work. It's fun. And I get to come in to this awesome dealership, meet a ton of new people that I try my best to take amazing care of, and make a heck of a lot of money doing it. The best part is, I'm not the only one that can do this. We all can. We just need to shift the perspective a little. Are you ready?

PRACTICAL APPLICATIONS

Align yourself with your customer's wants and needs. You're not selling them a car or a product for your benefit, you're selling them a car for them. Once you've come to really understand that, focus on improving your communication, asking the right questions, maintaining your enthusiasm, and finding solutions to their problems. Serve people wholeheartedly, and watch as this world of abundance begins to serve you.

CHAPTER 10
HOW TO START YOUR DAY

Do you have a long commute to work??? Are you stuck in horrible bumper to bumper traffic for most of it, surrounded by crazy drivers??? If so, then you're lucky! With the amazing technology available to us now, we can literally use that time to become masters of the universe...

Did you know that the most successful CEOs read an average of 60 BOOKS per year, learning and growing, expanding their perspectives, shifting their paradigms and standing on the shoulders of giants? You too, could use that time stuck in traffic reading tons and tons of books!!!! Well, not literally reading them... since you'll probably end up dead trying to drive and turn pages at the same time. But check it out, I have an Audible Account with the Platinum Monthly Membership. This gives me two book credits per month, a whopping 30% OFF on additional purchases made within that month, and TWO FREE Audible Original Titles, all for only $22.95 per month, which totals out to $276 per year! And for those of you that think that that's too expensive… believe this instead! It's way too expensive to NOT invest that little in yourself. I've literally made hundreds of thousands of dollars as a result of all of the books I've listened to on my commute, day in and day out! And from all of the stuff I'm learning in these books and the future books I will listen to, I promise to turn those into millions. If it weren't for all of those valuable lessons I've learned from so many amazing people before me, I wouldn't be nearly as successful as I am now!

Think about it. If you're surrounded by the same people every day, doing pretty much the same things over and over again, with the occasional mishaps that become the bigger events in your life, how in the world will anything change for you? Will you continue waiting for a miracle to happen?

Maybe win the lottery… invest early in the next Google or Amazon? Unlikely. The truth is, you'll probably cycle, living the same life over and over again. And if you're super satisfied and completely happy with how your life is going right now, then cool… but if you feel like there's so much more this world can offer… there is… but how will you tap into it?

Good thing is, if you're reading this book, you're either at the beginning stages of coming to realize how valuable reading and learning is, or you already know! (Unless someone gave you this book and is forcing you to read it) Either way, I'm hoping that by the end of it, something will change in you. Whether it's something big… or just that small tiny change that you needed to improve your life.

Start your day LEARNING!!! Then try to practice what you learn throughout your day. I can't tell you how powerful the application of learned knowledge becomes. It becomes a part of you… so much so that when you experience the power of it, you're left wanting to share it! How great would it be if we could all start sharing the wonderful things we learn instead of being one of the guys standing on the lot waiting for the next up, wasting your breath talking shit about other people or complaining about how boring it is, how bad this job sucks, or how broke you are.

Not only that, can you imagine what it's like to be a customer being greeted by a salesman who's just spent the last hour talking a ton of shit, being negative about every thing, and quickly plastering on a fake smile to try and break your guard down?

Now picture what it would be like being greeted by a professional who's just spent the past hour being uplifted by the amazing things that they've learned and applied… being greeted by that certain type of someone with a huge smile, who seems like they always fight to see the silver lining in even the darkest of clouds… You're probably gonna end up wanting to do business with that guy! See, that's who I've spent the past three years trying my best to become. And when I finally became that guy... I realized that that's who I truly was all along. That's who we *all* truly are... we've just been taught a lot of things that have trapped us into a cemented state of mind. That's why reading is so important. It lets you see life from so many more wonderful perspectives outside of the limits of yours. And once you begin opening your eyes and broadening your horizons, you'll have a better understanding of people.

You'll end up growing out of your own personal judgements against others, and in turn, find the freedom of no longer feeling like you're being judged. It takes you to a place of deep confidence... where you can finally break down your insecurities, expand your creativity, and allow yourself to connect with people at a whole 'nother level... one where the business of sales becomes so, so easy, that not only is it monetarily rewarding, but it's even more so emotionally and spiritually.

And if you've been in sales for awhile now, then you've experienced this wonderful state of feeling like you're making a sale with every customer you talk to. Sometimes, it lasts for a week... or much longer if you end up having one of those killer months. Listen to me... this is what it's like ALL THE TIME when you finally tap into your greatest self, serving others.

PRACTICAL APPLICATIONS

Get an Audible account. Download books that deal with personal development. Listen to them, then practice what you hear. If you prefer reading words off of paper, then do that. Whatever your preference, take in the knowledge and LEARN LEARN LEARN.

CHAPTER 11
COME TO WORK TO WORK!

So seriously, is it really ALL THE TIME? Does that mean I don't go through a couple dry spells where I'm not making a sale every single day? Again, if the metric is measured by making a sale or no sale, then yes, even I go through a couple days where I'm not selling someone a car... but if we are measuring it based on how I am showing up day in and day out, then I am crushing it, ALL THE TIME!

But to do this requires a foundational discipline that you cannot waver from. Look, you have to come to work to really WORK. Mark Cuban, a prominent, self made billionaire, owner of the Dallas Mavericks who started out as a bartender says, "It's not about money or connections — it's the willingness to outwork and outlearn everyone." You can't spend your time outside smoking cigarettes, socializing, gossiping, complaining, watching TV, playing video games or fooling around if you want to excel. Think of it this way, add any of those actions up together and what do they equal for you??? Let's do the math, complaining plus fooling around, plus a little gossiping, well it definitely does not equal a car deal. Now I get it. If you've been in the car business for any amount of time, then you know that there are periods where it seems like there's nothing to do. It's slow, there's no leads coming in, no fresh customers walking onto your dealership, and every one is feeling it! And this doesn't only happen in the car business, it's part of the territory with any thing sales or retail related… unless you happen to work at the Apple Store. LOL. But seriously, I'm guessing even they probably have some slow times where their showroom is completely dead. Okay, maybe not. At least not whenever I go into an Apple store to buy something. They're always busy! But BACK to what I was talking about. I get it. There is a lot of dead time in the car business. And that's every single day. It's what you DO during those dead times that makes the difference!

So here's a quick shout out to one of the best Used Car Managers I've ever worked with, Ted Vaughan… I used to think I was a pretty hard worker even though there were seasons of my sales career where I spent the dead times heavily binging on Netflix or Hulu. If I wasn't watching the fifth straight episode of Prison Break, I'd be outside chatting it up with the other bored sales people. On top of that, I'd even leave the dealership a bunch of times to go to the bank, get some groceries, grab some food and run personal errands, and even then, I still felt like I was a hard worker. Shoot, in my mind, I had to be… I was still their top producer. But truth is, I was fucking off quite a bit. I'll never forget the day Ted Vaughan had everyone take a full piece of paper, write down, "Am I doing the most productive thing I could be doing right now?" crumple it up, and put it in our pockets. That's a full 8 and a half by eleven sheet of paper. You know how uncomfortable that is to have sitting in your slim fit slacks? Man, did that change my work life and how I showed up on a daily basis. Actually, moment by moment basis because from this point on in my life, I had to constantly ask the question, "AM I DOING THE MOST PRODUCTIVE THING I COULD BE DOING RIGHT NOW?" And if I wasn't, well, it was time to do something else…

And as with any trade, coming to work with the right tools helps get the job done as efficiently as possible. It can even help during the times where things don't go quite as smoothly as you hoped. Short cuts and quick fixes might cover up a problem for a short while, but they never really get the job done right… the proper set of tools will.

So for a super successful, happy and holistically rewarding career in sales, you need to make sure you have the right tools in your tool box when you come to work. This also means you have to keep the bad tools like lying, manipulation, and fear tactics out. Here are the ones that I keep in mine… the most important of which brings us back full circle to chapter one.

HONESTY. If you compromise this part of it, then the majority of everything I've shared with you in this book will fall apart. It will literally be like building your house on sand. But don't get discouraged just yet! If up to this point, you've been someone who fibbed a little here, fibbed a little there, and have been getting by... WORK ON MASTERING THIS TOOL! In EVERY area of your life, and watch how much better everything becomes.

HUMILITY. This is one of the tools that I had a tendency of leaving at home, or in the car, or anywhere else but where it needed to be and it took me a very long time before I realized how important it was to have with me at all times. I can't tell you how powerful this tool actually is, it's one that you actually have to experience to understand what it can do. In the world of sales, interacting with managers and bosses, customers and co-workers, egos have a way of constantly getting in the way. Regardless where you stand in the hierarchy, USE THIS TOOL and humble yourself. When you learn how to use it properly, you can sit back and watch the magic happen.

PATIENCE. Becoming super successful doesn't happen overnight. And even once you become super successful, there's always the next big goal... however, none of those happen overnight neither. So you need to make sure you use this tool all the time, otherwise, you can end up irritable when expectations aren't met.

DILIGENCE. Take the time to do what you do well, and do it well, persistently.

So what's your process? What set of tools do you use? How do you show up to work every day? Do you bring all of your problems with you? Are you dying to tell everyone about your horrible girlfriend, how drunk you got, or how broke you are? Or are you dialed in and ready to go?

At my dealership, the processes are very simple. Do your follow up. Make your calls, send out emails, and text your customers. After you're done doing that, you can either sit outside and wait for an opportunity to come to you, or you can focus on creating your own opportunities. The problem is, this is the part where most people don't want to do the extra work.

On top of doing my daily follow up with leads and fresh customers, I contact at least 15–20 previous customers every single day… some, just to thank for their business, congratulate on their new car, wish a happy birthday or a happy anniversary to, and some that I call and ask for referrals from. Then, I hand write thank you cards, making nice personalized designs on the envelope, and send those out. After that, I post pictures of me and my happy customers on Facebook and Instagram. If I get done with all that and I'm still not working with a customer, then I'm taking pictures of one or two fresh trade ins to post onto Facebook Marketplace. See, if you add **any** of those actions together, you've got a high probability of those actions equaling a car deal. Do that every single day, and you're creating a momentum that can't be stopped… even during the slow seasons.

See, that's the thing… if you spend 80% of your time at work working, then you're going to reap a lot of benefits. Especially if you do this every single day. However, if you're like the majority of the sales people you work with, truly working only 20% of the time they're there, well, at this point, you can do the math. You're only going to be 20% successful, and that, for lack of a better word, simply sucks.

PRACTICAL APPLICATIONS

Whatever your profession, come to work to work. Do the remedial processes that you're required to do EVERY SINGLE DAY you're at the job. Don't allow yourself to slack off. If you want to rest, then rest… but only AFTER you've finished the things you need to do that day. That way, it doesn't pile up on you where it becomes too overwhelming to try and catch up. Stay ahead of the curve. Don't use shortcuts. And make sure you're using the right tools when you're going to work!

CHAPTER 12
A VISION STATEMENT
TO KEEP YOU GROUNDED

The late great Apple co-founder Steve Jobs, a man widely recognized as a pioneer of the microcomputer revolution, and the visionary genius behind the iPod, iPhone, and iPad once said, "If you are working on something exciting that you really care about, you don't have to be pushed. The vision pulls you." So let's see if you're even in the right place. Is sales exciting to you? Are you the type of person that's naturally confident enough to ask for anything and everything without being worried about being told, "No?" Do you enjoy the negotiation process or does it scare the heck out of you? Does closing a deal excite you? And I'm not talking just about the monetary reward of it... I'm talking about that super tough, hard to convince, indecisive buyer that after hours of grinding it out, you're finally able to "close," does that get your blood flowing? Also, is the product you're selling something you really care about? Do you truly and deeply believe in the product you're selling and the value it offers? Does the product provide solutions, joy, happiness, or advantages for your customers? If neither of this describes you or what you're selling, you might be in the wrong business. If you're only in sales because you think you can make a lot of money in it, sure… you'll probably make a lot of money doing it, but you'll have a high probability of being over-stressed and over-worked, and after awhile, you'll probably burn out. However, if the sales process and everything about it excites you, or the product you're selling is something you truly believe in, then let's put together a powerful vision statement that'll pull you towards your goal, backed by a mission statement that will continue to guide you through the ups and downs.

Before we do that, let's go over the differences between the two. A Vision Statement describes your desired future position for you or your company. What do you want to be in the future? Or what do you want your company to be in five, 10, or 15 years from now. This will be your roadmap, setting a defined direction for you or your company's growth! A Mission Statement describes what you're going to do NOW that falls in line with your vision, your goals, purpose and values. It's a formal summary that explains what you do, how you do it, and why you do it! A good mission statement can inspire the crap out of you, the company you work for, and the people around you!

Mine is very simple. My Mission is to provide an amazing life for my family by offering the very best service to each and every customer I talk to, a safe and reliable vehicle at a fair price, and treating every one of them with the utmost respect and care. My Vision is to be the Most Loved Car Salesman ever, helping other sales people turn into the most loved sales professional in their fields. Combined, they keep me focused and driven...

I don't own the company I work for, so my mission statement is specific for me, and not the company as a whole. I'm not even sure Boulder Hyundai has even written one out, and if they have, I might have missed it. Look, if your company has one, and you fully subscribe to it, then you're in the right place. But if you don't agree with it or if your company does not have one, make one for yourself that you DO believe in, or do something else! See, my personal mission is greater than selling cars. I mean, love the business... the negotiation process where I'm having a blast going back and forth with a really tough customer, solving problems, helping the credit challenged get into a safe and reliable vehicle when they never thought they could, getting someone their first car, taking care of friends and family, and then taking care of the friends and family they send me... I love it all, but my mission is bigger than that.

The mission that really keeps me moving is my family. And not just to provide for them... this business has already covered that for me, as it can for you and your family. However, my mission is to provide an AMAZING life... one of abundance and love. One that I can be proud of, and enjoy with my wife and my daughter. A life that not only financially supports me, but emotionally, and spiritually helps me grow. And how do I do that? By providing the VERY BEST CUSTOMER SERVICE possible to each and every single customer I talk to. By being fair with the pricing, without ripping people off. By treating each and every one of them with the utmost respect and care. And this means everyone. Not just the people I like. If I limited it to just the people I like, or the people I think I can make money from, I am missing out on so much more of the rewards and fulfillment that comes in many other forms.

My Vision Statement, though it may sound grandiose, cocky, and silly, is really my bigger vision! To be the MOST LOVED CAR SALESMAN. Shoot, it's the hashtag I post with each and every single picture of me and my customers, and it's how I've branded myself. However, it's not me saying I'm the best or anything like that… Like I said in the earlier chapters, the only way to be the most loved car salesman is by being the most lov*ING*. That means being the most honest, caring, car salesman that's consistently willing to go above and beyond to take care of my customers! And with every experience and lesson I learn, I want to share that with all of you so that you, too, can be the most loved "Whatever" salesman in your neck of the woods! I want all of you to be able to live a rich, abundant life — I want you all to be emotionally and spiritually filled, loving and caring for the people around you. I want everyone one of you who's working in sales enjoying your job, and making the best out of every day that you're working and selling. Do you realize that the average American will spend 90,000 hours of their life at their job? Might as well do something you love doing, with integrity, serving others, and getting paid ridiculously for your efforts.

So do yourself a huge favor. Start asking yourself the following questions: What do you do? How do you do it? And most importantly, WHY do you do it? And once you figure that out, what do you want to be in the future? What kinds of values will be rooted in what you do and who you want to become? Instead of wasting so much time worrying, ponder these types of thoughts, and watch how drastically your life can change. Truth is, if you spend most of your time worrying, then a lot of the things you worry about tend to come true. But if you replace the time you spend worrying with thinking about who and what you want to be... then you'll come up with the amazing answers... I mean, if you don't ask, you'll never get the answers, right? So start asking them... every free chance you get. Ask.

PRACTICAL APPLICATIONS

Ask yourself the questions. Discover your purpose. Write out your mission statement.

CHAPTER 13
THE POWER OF VISUALIZATION

By now, mostly every one has heard of the power of visualization. Books and movies like "The Secret" and the "Law of Attraction" have become pretty mainstream in the last decade, with tons of other authors including the concepts in their books and coaching modalities. But if for some reason, you've been hiding under a rock, let me give you my version of what it is, and how it has worked for me.

Visualization is the process of taking the time to imagine and specify what it is you want, with the intentions of making them come true. There's a million different ways of doing this from meditating, affirmations, light therapy, writing it down, breathing it in, etc. etc. but I'm narrowing this down to my personal experience with it, and what I realized with the different methods I tried, and the thought processes that went along with them.

I'm a huge "to-do-list" maker, and if there's anything I'm about to do that would be more efficiently done with a list, then a list was definitely going to be made. At work, I start my day with that list, especially if there's a lot of extra things that need to get done, and I don't want to have to waste any extra energy or mental bandwidth trying to remember each one of them.

Now when I first read about the Law of Attraction, and The Secret, I thought it would be super easy. If I think it and focus hard enough on it, it would happen, right? But for most of us who have tried this method, it doesn't just happen right away. There's a long period of time in between the "thinking it" and the "imagined outcome," and what we do during that time can really mess it up for us.

I remember going into work, writing out my to-do-lists, and on the first lines, write out how grateful I was to have this amazing job and all the blessings it provided. The next lines followed up with all of the things I needed to do that day. The first item on that list was "Sell a car," followed by 2. Do your follow up, 3. Send out thank you cards, 4. Post customer pictures on Facebook, and whatever else I needed to do. For me, it was GREAT when I would be able to highlight every one of those tasks, especially if it included the only task on the list that I couldn't fully control on my own — selling a car. If that happened, I would go home feeling super accomplished.

But what happened during the times I didn't sell a car? I've already spent the time visualizing that I would ... so what went wrong? Did I do the visualizations wrong? Did I not include the "feeling" of selling a car in my meditation? Is "the secret" even real? What if the secret is that it's all just a big joke? What can I do to make sure that the next time I visualize it, it happens?

These were some of the thoughts that would send me spiraling down. And if I ended up going a few days without selling a car, then the thoughts deteriorated even worse to the point where I would say "screw it" for a couple days before trying the whole process all over again. Unfortunately, this created even more resistance from me being able to receive what I wanted.

What I realized was that it wasn't HOW I was visualizing that screwed it all up for me, it was WHAT I was visualizing that created the biggest disconnect. I was visualizing SELL-ING A CAR. But if I really take a step back and look at that, that's just a selfish want that could possibly affect what a cus-tomer was intending for themselves. Hear me out. What if a customer's intention was ONLY to get more information on a vehicle, feel how it drives to see if they like it, and look into some of the numbers to see if it was affordable to them? What if that's ALL THAT THEY WANTED from coming into the dealership? Well, if my visualization is simply focused on selling them a car, then there's already a huge disconnect. You know that feeling you get when a customer comes on the lot and tells you they're not going to buy today, they're just look-ing? Well, that's probably the same feeling they get when you approach them with the notion of, I'm just here to sell you a car so I can get paid. This concept really got me thinking.

See, I know the power of visualization. It's worked for me in miraculous ways already. Some that I realized only AFTER it happened, and some where I knowingly used it going in. For example, I tore my shoulder's AC joint in a mountain biking accident. The doctors suggested I get it operated on, otherwise, I will forever have a hanging shoulder and would only be able to regain 80% of my strength back without it. During this time, I had been reading books like "Becoming Supernatural," by Dr. Joe Dispenza, and hearing about how athletes would train for the Olympics by visualizing themselves doing the activities, and how the brain couldn't tell the difference.

Three days after the accident, I was back in the gym with a sling on, right side immobilized, but working out with my left side. As I was working out my left side, I would meditate and visualize that my right side was working out with it, and that it was getting stronger as it was healing. Fast forward to today, I am now stronger than I was before even having the accident, so I know this stuff really works!

See, if a customer came in with intention to buy a car, and met with my intention to sell them a car, then there was no disconnect, and the outcome flowed easily. However, if a customer simply came in to gather information, and my intention was to sell them a car, then there would be that huge disconnect. So what if I shifted my visualization? What if I created a vision that would serve everyone involved?

So here's what I was thinking... every customer who comes on my lot wants to be well taken care of and treated with respect. Every customer who comes on my lot with questions wants to have them answered by a professional, as opposed to an opinionated idiot who didn't take the time to learn the products they're trying to sell. And every customer who comes on my lot that's ready to buy wants to be treated fairly and get a good deal. So what if I shifted my visualization to meet theirs?

What if I visualized myself taking care of every single customer who walks into my lot and treating them with respect? What if I visualized myself answering questions professionally, or getting them answers to the questions I didn't know, and in my case, doing it with good energy, enthusiasm, and a smile? And instead of visualizing how much money I can make off of a single deal, what if I visualized offering a fair price with the highest level of service to each and every customer who was ready to buy?

So that's exactly what I did and the outcomes have been amazing. I have so many happy customers, and I am getting paid ridiculously well for taking care of them. The best part is, I've turned this super stressful job of car sales into such a fun and rewarding vocation that I don't even feel like I'm working half the time. Shoot, if we're going to spend 90,000 plus hours of our lives working, we might as well enjoy it!

I hope that this book has inspired you to do the same!

PRACTICAL APPLICATIONS

Read this book a couple times. Maybe something new will jump out at you every time you read it. But please understand, this book is just an overview. This isn't a step by step process that you can follow. Rather, it is a glimpse of how amazing and abundant your life can be serving others.